The Wine of Astonishment

Poems

*To: Linda Lee
with appreciation for her
writing, her teaching and
exquisite kindness*
— *Ed Harris*

W. Edward Harris

W. Edward Harris

Outskirts Press, Inc.
Denver, Colorado

The Wine of Astonishment
Poems

Outskirts Press, Inc.
http://www.outskirtspress.com

ISBN: 978-1-4327-4982-8

Outskirts Press and the "OP" logo are trademarks belonging to Outskirts Press, Inc.

PRINTED IN THE UNITED STATES OF AMERICA

"Thou hast shown thy people hard things:
thou hast made us to drink the wine of astonishment."

Psalm 60, verse 3

Table of Contents

From Shoes	1
Singing to Salamanders	3
Going North, Lost	4
Cortez at Iztapalapa	7
Hawk	9
Cave of Blind Fish	11
Watcher	12
Blue Pigeon	14
Magic City	16
Birmingham, 1947	18
Subversive Sundays	19
A World Gone Missing	21
JoJo's Gun Shop	23
We Stood In Slushy Snow	25
Every Day	27
Girls Disappear	28
King's Blood	29
Mystery of Plums	31
Lies of the Poets	34
The Thing that Sings	37
Test Question	38
Morsel	39
Body of Words	41
Buying My Coffin	44
After She Went Away	46
Under My Mother's Pillow	48
Star in My Blue Heaven	50

Katrina, Unfolding   51

The Green Jar   53

Jocasta   55

Stone Lion   58

Yunnan Triple Delight   60

Day on Red Mountain   61

The Art of Shining Shoes   63

Continental Connection Flight 3407   64

Baton   66

Terminal Madness   68

Altered Life   72

The Dead Show   75

Gift   78

Ride of Her Life   79

Veil of Silence   82

Red Memory   84

Staggered   85

From Shoes

Everyone is from somewhere and me?
I am from shoes, shoes set food on our table.
shoes put clothes on our back. The smell of
polished leather shoes is the perfume
that carries all my history. Anything I have
ever done has had shoes in it, save the tender
moments of sex but it always preceded by
the kicking off of her shoes and then mine.

Shoes have the smell of cash and the thousand
feet I've lifted and shoe-horned into the shoe
that was their destiny, their dancing shoes,
their wedding shoes, their looking-for-a-job
shoes, their running shoes, their shoes for
Nepal and the assault on the great mountain.
Dress shoes for church, work shoes with steel
toes for the iron workers of my hometown.

I got married in a special order pair of sleek
black calf John C. Robert's 9 1/2-C French
toe shoes to a girl wearing white patent leather
flats, size 6 1/2 at the First Christian Church
on a steamy June night. After a reception
we traveled to the Holiday Inn for our honey-
moon but were up the next morning opening
the store at nine, cleaning off the front all

gooey and goo-goo eyed smirky that we now
knew the secret of life and it wasn't all work.
We sold some shoes that day, the register
ringing and ringing and we were on our way
living the life of hard work our parents laid
out but we were putting our own shine on it.

Singing to Salamanders

Out in the falling leaf woods,
singing to the trees and salamanders,
I study the spider's intricate handiwork—
where cicadas and dragonflies are buzzing
yet held fast waiting to be dinner.
My dog, unleashed is barking mad
to be in these woods. If he heard a
pack howling all our training would
be ignored as he ran toward the sound.
Instead, he brings me a hunk of fur
of some long dead small animal.
He is wanting a pocket treat and a pat.
I sing to snakes slithering toward hibernation
and half-clothed trees dancing in the sun.

Going North, Lost

It came in a rush, no warning,
a wind-ripping tornado first day
of deer season. It was my first
hunt with the men. We set up camp
on wet ground around Hatchet Creek.
I was 15, the good boy, already
spoken of as "the preacher."
That first night we huddled in the
tent, smoke stinging our eyes eating
barbecue, beans, potatoes and
white bread sopping the red sauce.
We played poker and the men drank,
deliberately skipping me as the
bottle was passed mouth to mouth.

Next morning I sat in deer blind set
in a tree hiding from the deer who were
already on the run from the blasts of
first day of the season. Charlie Austin
manager of the Western Auto Store
came with me. He had a fine new rifle.
Waiting was boring, we had to be quiet
so as not to scare the deer. We ate our
lunch sandwiches at nine o'clock. He
sneaked little sips from a pint of whiskey
that I pretended not to see. He decided to
give up the wait and go back to camp
leaving all the deer that might show up to me.

I stayed until, the sun high in the sky,
a deer came into view, a twelve point
buck, beginner's luck, they called it.

Filled with fear and tension I startled
and then fired, not a killshot, instead,
a wounding. He dropped to the ground,
then struggled to his feet and ran leaping
the downed logs and bushes on the wet ground.
I followed blindly, tracking him through
beat-back brush and bloody spotted trail
through steady wind-whipped rain,
determined not to lose my deer.

After an hour he went to ground, oozing blood.
I came upon him lying under a bush
in downy hollowed out nest, panting.
Exhausted I lay down beside him for his warmth,
feeling his heart surge and gurgle.
Full of death fear I hugged him, my
sad search ended.

In the weakness of the dying day sun
I rose, shouldered my deer staggering
under the weight, his blood mingling
with my sweat and the lightly falling rain,
the wind easy now at my back.
Boy, rifle and deer stumbled across the field.

I slogged out to the blacktop.
rejoicing as the hard surface steadied my feet,
the deer bowing my neck,
weary muscles trembling,
tears threatening my collapse.
Searching cousins and uncles
found me, going north, lost.

We ate venison stew that evening.
Around the campfire the saga
was told by the men who found me.
How I was dragging the rifle,
weaving like a drunk under the
burden of the twelve point hart,
blood soaking into my down jacket,
blood in my shoes squishing
as I walked, my dazed look

and dirt all over me, all laughingly exposed.
When the Four Roses passed that night I was
invited to drink the bitter liquor they believed
a man needs to ease the pain of being a man.

Cortez at Iztapalapa

Birds are more beautiful than art.
In a landscape of chalked sunlight.
Songbirds nest in low trees.
You can reach out to them.
Dustless is the air at Lake Chalco.
The people stride with feathers
on their feet, hands and head.
Cortez' steel-helmeted invaders
are surprised by the colors
in the vine-woven aviaries:
the green jays, golden tanagers,
flycatchers, wrens blue, yellow and red,
black herons, white ibis, egrets, canaries,
parakeets, large red, green and purple
parrots, blue throated hummingbirds
dancing with red and white camellias.

These are public aviaries maintained for
beauty, variety, joy and public honor.
The gold seeking Spaniards have come
demanding tribute. It is June 16, 1521
the army pauses, torches are lit, a long
moment of silence and then Cortez
orders the aviaries set afire.
Squawks, flaming shrill unworldly shrieks
of thousands of birds, choking smoke
and tang of burned flesh rises upwards
over the screaming wing-flopping panic.
Feathers rain down to cover the lake.
Even the Spaniards weep.

Hawk

I saw the grass moving. Wind.

Then the odd white tips of feathers,
a hawk is down in the stubbled field.

Overhead two hawks circle.

The grounded bird is dead, movement
only from the wind, the wings ruffling
five feet across fanning, opening.

The hawk on its back is
all beak and clawed feet,
those wings attached to so small
a body it defies proper design.

I see his eyes—
he looks at me
from the hawk place of the dead.

"Hail, hawk, prince of winds."

Strange. No sign of foul play.
He is not shot. Poisoned perhaps.

I go to the house for gloves,
a knife and a plastic bag.

When I lift him his wings heave
open as if to take flight.
Icy fear sails through my body.

I place him reverently back upon
the roughed ground, ashamed
of wanting a feather trophy
desiring only his hawk spirit.

Cave of Blind Fish

There is a cave of blindfish.
Sudden, it comes, you may be
blind too at the bottom of some
cave. Like a child you breathe
the world, it shines for you.

The twin towers eat the planes
over and over again falling,
crashing, watching the dusty softness
spread over the city and world.
I grieve alone, I do not even have
ashes to rub into my wounded eyes.
I go for hours without crying,
Every minute people are dying
There are no angels larking about.
Damned poor angels if they are.

The whole house seems to be thinking,
The hunger that men are cannot be satisfied.
I damn those who advocate murder
as a way to improve the world.

Watcher

I

The abandoned child, the neglected child, the abused child
becomes a watcher, ever scanning the emotional horizon of his
keepers. Watching is a survival skill as natural as breathing to
one who is at the mercy of others.

II

Set before the television he watches, learning to do it quietly,
making himself small, quiet as a stone. The images flick from
screen into his imagination.
He likes Roadrunner who endures countless beatings, crashes
and falls but pops back—alive and whole, ready new for action.
He delights in all those with superpowers—Mighty Mouse
especially—flying to help others. More than anything he wants
to be strong and help others.

III

At school he sees Robert on crutches and helps him
with his books and opens doors.
He reads to Douglas for whom the black print is a puzzle.
Carl Steiner, the one called Jew, gets beaten and he goes to help
him and gets hit for his trouble. He wants to know what Jew
means. Is he one?

IV

He does not understand why a three-legged dog is funny.
He does not understand why boys spit water on the girls.
He does not understand why Raymond Ewing is always tripped.

V

He reads the papers and comes to know the pain of the world
is so much greater than his own.
He watches and knows he did not have to wear the yellow star
or drop his mother's hand as they take different paths to the
showers of gas.

VI

He watches suffering that goes on for years. He watches Burt
Sheffield who got polio and drags his leg in pain through the
halls at Glen Iris school.

VII

He watched Marlys Schwartz whose father used her for sex and
other nastiness until she hanged herself in her basement. He
is the one who saw her naked body through the window. Mrs.
Schwartz gave him a dollar not to tell anyone what he saw. He
never does tell but is full of fear knowing that God knows. He
watches for God but God never shows.

Blue Pigeon

They flew the skies of the Ohio Valley darkening
the world. Settlers, farmers, preachers saw them as
an ominous portent of apocalypse.

Close up its head was blue-gray, its back
and wings like weathered wood, an earthy
blue—they called it Blue Pigeon.

Audubon observed a flock that blotted out
the sun for eight hours as millions passed down
the Ohio River in whirling numberless beauty.

The immense flock whirred thunderously.
It was unlike anything ever heard until the
invention of the great electric turbines.

They devoured massive amounts of acorns,
beechnuts, chestnuts, insects and planted corn.
stirring fear in the hearts of farmers.

The Blue Pigeon was found to be tasty.
They fetched a fancy price in New York and
Boston chefs served them with exquisite sauces.

They were so easily shot, a fool could feed
his family and earn a living providing pigeon
to the urban masses who never fired a gun.

Hunters tied decoy pigeons on a stump,
(the original *stool pigeons*), along with tons
of corn, acorns and nuts spread upon the ground.

When the flock landed hunters opened fire with
pistols, shotguns, rifles, and Gatling guns.
The slaughter was remorseless, relentless.

When attacked the pigeons did not fly away
but stayed cooing and soothing their dying
mates only to be shot themselves.

There were in 1820, perhaps five billion,
of these rainbow dusted birds. Decades of hunting
brought the numbers down toward extinction.

The last of these pigeons were a pair carefully cared
for named George and Martha Washington, major
attractions at the Cincinnati Zoo after 1900.

When George died, the widowed Martha was
on display daily to the burly bustling crowds
that came unendingly to see the last Blue Pigeon.

It was cloudy and overcast the day of her death
September 1, 1914—as war was breaking out in
Europe beginning our century of total war.

Magic City

Before it was America's problem child
Birmingham was a fantasy of wealth and jobs.
The coming of the railroads, iron ore, limestone
and coal set the stage for a boomtown of
the New South with its glowing factories.
Thousands came to dig the ore, limestone and coal
to mill steel, pig iron, fabricate valves,
fittings, and to supply the mines and factories:
selling lumber to uphold the mineshafts, picks,
buckets, shovels, to get the ore and coal. They
lay steel rails. built houses, put up great hotels,
sold liquor and furnished entertainment as well as
a few discreet establishments for sex. Everybody
had a chance to be pioneer and make some money.
They could worship the only God they knew, a rough,
hard God who dealt harshly with his chosen people.
Temples, tabernacles and tents went up to
hold the crowds in need of salvation.
Minor sects heralded redemption by Jesus'
precious blood promising the gift of tongues.
Birmingham was a city of hope, its light shining
out into the Black Belt cotton fields.
Blacks speeded their pace when they saw
the black serpentine smoke coming out of
smokestacks which meant a new life and independence.
No more working for Mr. Charlie up in the big house.

No more sharecropping, staring up a mule's ass
ten hours a day planting cotton, fighting the boll weevil,
ending the year just a little less in debt than you started.
Here a man could get work and at the end of the
week, cash and Saturday night.
It was not Bad Birmingham then but a Magic City,
with streetcars to ride, lights and paved streets.
Birmingham cast its light to Italy, Syria, Greece,
Hungary, Poland, Bohemia and men who knew
how to dig coal and iron from the earth came
carrying family pictures, icons, birth certificates,
starched white shirts, boots and hope
in crammed suit cases bound with rope.
Fine neighborhoods were platted, parks laid out,
schools, trains, streetcars tied the city together.
A city of crystalline water, where the Appalachian spring
astonished when crabapple and dogwood burst
beribboned, braided, perfumed. Tulips jump up in yards
as in a musical. Yellow forsythia flourish as fireworks,
a democracy of decoration, adorning villas, gated subdivisions
shacks and trailer courts with chained barking dogs.

Birmingham, 1947

Hard city, mean city, men and women are fed
to the greedy coal, iron and steel Moloch.
Magic City of Iron with a glass jaw, where
"Good times stays shortest, hard times stays longest."

A Black city, a White city.
Warnings: watch where you sit,
watch where you walk or
drink and watch your mouth.

City of churches and gospel singers selling little Jesus.
City pregnant with labor violence and racial bombings.
City of ineffectual civic clubs, drowsing over lunch.
City where police and Klan-fear ruled with razor, guns and dogs.
City of false memory of a magnolia-scented way of life.
City where no one seems to notice the choking smoky air.
City of Ku Klux white-robed, dunce-capped wizards.
City of beauty contests, every girl a Southern Belle.
City of Vulcan atop Red Mountain in the cleanest air.
City with a jail fabled in song famously always filled.

Subversive Sundays

Sundays were subversive, all weekday
values and practices, set aside, even attacked.
In my divided city of nigger, kike, wop, honky, and redneck,
this white boy listened to broadcasts of black churches with
their gospel singers, quartets, choirs, sultry saxophones,
dancing organs, prancing pianos and trumpet-bending notes.

I let the confusing foreign sound of it baptize me.
Sin was named and dramatized, given its name and its due—
shameless bootleggers, wanton widows, drinking men, men who
won't work, robbing, stealing, cheating, back door men,
playing the numbers, dicing, shooting, fucking and fighting.

These were not the tepid sins I knew like
not reading your Bible, being late for church,
not having prepared the lesson, not staying for church,
being late for school, failing your chores
but sin real and glorious. met with sharpest condemnations,
the preacher puffing and whooping, pounding the pulpit,
armed with the Bible, armed with the Gospel, clothed in
whole armor of God, he did battle with Devil, God's
favorite angel, the great Prince of Darkness.

This was no cute cartoon devil but a shape-shifting,
smooth talking, conscience-easing pleader of pleasures assuring
the sinner: "No one will know. You deserve it. Take it!"

My pretty little white Jesus, sweet to a fault
could reject Satan's temptations, could turn away,
but he could never wrestle the bastard to the ground, and whip his ass.
His Daddy couldn't even do that. Devil was sly, mean and tough.
It took a powerful voiced preacher, hollering, praying, gathering
the power of the whole congregation singing, shouting
until finally, in a crescendo of organ and trumpet they run the lying,
lascivious son of a bitch demon from the church making room
for The Holy Ghost. Then shouting over and over
"Thank you, Jesus! Thank you, Jesus!" dazed people
fall out fainting, while the organ leaps bippity-bop-bop-bop
punctuating the victory, the uprising of Jesus and his people.

A World Gone Missing

I take Car 22 from Tarrant City, rattle through
Boyles, Inglenook, East Birmingham, Norwood.
I get a whiff of methane flame-off at Alabama By-Products
a great prosperous fart blanketing our world.
Next, Donovan Coffee Company's roasting follows
us all the way down Tenth Avenue to Linde Air.
Then baking sweet rolls at McGough's Bakery,
then the nose-stinging molten steel at Sloss.
then the tang of cast iron pipe, the ground smoking.
then the milky sweet curdle of Melrose Creamery's
Ice Cream: "Made Its Way by the Way its Made."
Perfume blasts onto the sidewalks at Loveman's.
I go into Rosenberger's Birmingham Trunk Factory
to see the Big Red Elephant and smell the leathers.
Next door at Kinney's, the aroma of shoes and polish
and the smell of people's feet trying them on.
The smell of scented hotdogs and kraut slides out
of Tom's Hole In the Wall, men elbow to elbow.
At Kress popping corn butters the whole store.
At The Alabama "Showplace of the South"

sweat, Old Spice and Chanel No. 5 fight it out.
Linseed oil essence rises from the floors
at Phillips High School, the very smell of learning.
The pushcart man hawks his wares in staccato tattoo
"Hot Tamales! Hot Tamales! Hot Tamales! Hot!"
I get one to breathe in the cayenne-peppered delicacy
wrapped in greasy corn shucks, its red juice dripping.
I'll carry the stain and odor with me forever.
Afternoon brings the smell of news, ink and newsprint,
The library's leathery foxed volumes exude acrid dust.
There's the aromatic promise of the new stacked on
the counters of Smith and Hardwick Books.
Funky savor of fetid garbage as the truck rolls to a stop.
Smell of barbecue cooked all day overspreads the city
announcing the evening, proclaiming the glorious
supper of pig. "Yas, suh, it's cooked in de pit!"
Birmingham with its colors, sounds and smells,
a world gone missing cries out over the years
to my memory locked and loaded and lost.

JoJo's Gun Shop

She sells cell phones
at the Galleria.

Twenty-four—no husband,
she has two boys.

Some break-ins,
shootings on her street
make her think:
"I need a gun."

Passing

JoJo's
      Stop & Go
      Gun Shop:

"Guns Cheaper Than
      a Tank of Gas,"

She stops, knocks
and is admitted.

She asks to see
the clerk's holstered pistol.

He hands it to her,
it fires, she dies.
They say:

"Guns don't kill people."

Her sons, 3 & 5,
go home to grandma's now.

We Stood In Slushy Snow

Cars splashed the greasy slurry
onto our little crew.

We've come to bear witness for the man
who was shot on the Village Pantry parking lot.
He fell dead beside pump number three.

We have to stand off the premises as
corporate does not permit praying or
demonstrations on its property.

The 26-year old black man was shot with
a Glock automatic, one second, nine holes
another black man dead in urban America.

Vibrating through the Christmas air is music
hip-hop and rap tunes muffled and throbbing
bloomb   bloomb   bloomb!

Mother says: "John was a good boy."
His girl friend, their daughter pressed close
against the cold, watches, says nothing.

One of the trained grief counselors begins
the all-purpose prayer for these occasions.
Before he is done the black windowed

SUV with John's curious friends slows
as it comes our way again, trying to see
what is happening, what is going on.
bloomb   bloomb   bloomb!

Our intention: To acknowledge this death and
sanctify this icy murder spot for the dead
man, his child, his family, the community.

We sprinkle the blessed and scented holy
water into the snow and slather pungent
oil over the icy ground making a cross.

Mother says: "I am glad someone cares."
The truck with black glass comes again:
Bloomb   bloomb   bloomb!

Every Day

They are shot down in alleys
in crack houses, outside bars,
coming out of food markets,
in the parking lots of Wal-Mart,
Shell, CVS, Village Pantry,
Best Buy, and Kroger.
Young black men, many
already fathers in their teens,
handsome, beautiful as only
the young can be.
Ninety thousand died on the
streets, alleys, parking lots
of America in the 1990s, ten
years, nine thousand a year.
Ten times the number ever
lynched in a hundred years
or shot by the police or
martyred in the civil rights
movement for freedom and justice.

Trouble is, no one seems to care.
It was another black man who
pulled "the trigger on the nigger."
Nobody tells The Man nothing—no
rats on these mean streets just
murderers and the murdered.
What is killing our young men?

Girls Disappear

Dogs brought the bone home.
It proved to be a human forearm
belonging to Shawntelle Williams.

She was not reported missing.
Nobody knew she was gone.
Girls disappear all the time.

No one could be found
to claim the rest of the body
dug up on a Tuxedo Street lot.

In the city, bodies are found
on vacant lots, in garbage cans,
dumpsters, empty apartments.

There are many dead living
in the city. They just don't
make as much noise or trouble.

King's Blood

It is September 15 again,
hot, the sun barely up,
a promise of Fall in the air,
first high school football night.

I walk to get the newspaper
at the bottom of my drive where
the newsboy has carelessly tossed
it, no concern for an old man.

"Three Killed in West End." Gang war
over drugs and turf. Two boys and a six-year
old girl designated "collateral damage."
Gang colors will decorate the caskets.

Next story: sixteen-year old boy
shot robbing a Quik Stop. He had
a gun but so did the manager.
Protests possible. I lay the paper aside.

My mind goes to the lines he spoke
at the funeral forty years ago
"All things work together for the good
for them that love the Lord."

That was his text for the eulogy
for the four Sunday School girls
who were bombed in the church.
I was doubtful then, angered to hear it.

Something greater must be said,
some action, some redemption,
not those old words of stoic acceptance,
affirming whatever is, is right.

He kept the town from exploding though.
Five years later gunfire in his ears he died.
Tears flooded when I saw his room at the
Lorraine Motel—stunned by what is lost.

Mystery of Plums

"There is a view that poetry should improve your life.
I think people confuse it with the Salvation Army."

-John Ashbery

Do not confuse
poetry with the
Salvation Army.

Nor is it a
newspaper
or a blog
full of inside dope,
or aromatherapy,
or a good massage.

It is not a garden
or a record of Buddha's
enlightenment,
Jesus'subtle teachings.

Although it is
parables, wild stories,
accounts of inner
and outer weather,
the juiciness of
peaches, the mystery
of plums and mangoes,
the taste of macaroons
and tawny sherry,
complaints,
whines
bitches,
brags.

You will find accounts of
the wisdom and foolishness
of mothers,
fathers,
praise of the roiling sun,
lots of rain, blizzards and
snow storms, camellias,
coneflower, oaks,
white pine, tulip poplars.
anguished longings,
unrealized desperate hopes.

You'll meet oven birds,
beavers, hummingbirds,
eagles, vultures, hawks,
often symbolic,
and words antique
or just minted
that you may have to look up.

Poetry's trumpet sets
no armies marching,
but it has created more
than a few children.
It has touched the tender
parts of women and
the hard parts of men
who often care not
a whit for poetry.

Lies of the Poets

I had sex with a famous poet last night.
I don't even know how I got there.
She signed my book after the reading,
handing it back, her hand over mine,
mouthing the words "I want you."
After that we went for drinks, and then
bing, bang, boom here we are in her room
at the Ritz—I didn't know poets lived like
this on the road—its posh, flowers, baskets
of fruit, one of those liquor stocked refrigerators.

We drank the champagne undressing.
Later I say, "Barbie," (not her real name
I can't tell you her real name, she's very famous
renowned for poems about her husband),
 "I have to leave now." She rolls over and
says, her lips pouty: "Don't go baby.
Its not every night you get to have sex
with a famous poet." I agree but gush
uncontrollably "I'm married." She says
 "So am I, that makes us equal."
That convinced me so we go at it again.

I really like her, she didn't seem like a poet in bed
but rather like a woman who is used to having her
way with men. I never slept with a redhead before
but I think it was dyed. I notice how we got out of
our clothes, her bra is on the lamp, panties on a
door knob, blouse on the floor, red Mary Janes at both
ends of the room, the bottle is tangled in her
panty hose. My clothes are in a neat pile.
My cell phone flashes lighting the mirror.
I think of poor Lord Byron on his wedding night
watching the mirrored candles, crying "Surely I am in hell."

Her question interrupts my brown study.
"You don't think I'm slutty do you?"
"Hell, no." I say, "Sexually adventurous, maybe,
but definitely not slutty."
She liked that and said "You've got a way with words."
Yeah, I'm poet too, thinking what is this sex going to cost me?
Then we go at it again making the beast with two backs.
I could be home resting up to write some poems.
I wanted to ask her about some of her poems
or if she could maybe help me get published
but that seemed—you know *gauche.*

Maybe I'll be in one her poems, she'll write about anything.
I've been reading *Inferno*, so I ask if she knew Dante.
She thought musing, choosing her words carefully:
"I don't know. I know I never slept with him, I know that."
This bedroom comedy makes a little turn toward *undivine*.
Fear ripples up my spine as I think about that
second circle of hell and her husband who, I think
she said in one of her poems, duels with Samurai swords.
You'd know her name if I said it but I'm not one to kiss and tell.
She writes just like I want a poet to write,
free and easy, tropes like garments all over the place.

The Thing that Sings

The grass is choiring its love songs.
The Earth rolls through the firmament
intoning its quiet hymns of praise.
The stars in their courses harmonize
the steady hum of the Big Bang.
The daffodils, the lilies at Easter lift
their budded heads and they carol too.
There is a little rooted-dance they do.

I roll away the stone from the tomb
of despair and I rise, a green thing,
grateful for this day, singing like
the birds to all the muffled strangled voices
that we should be that thing that sings,
now at the beginning of creation.

Test Question

I do not know if the seasons remember their
history or if the days and nights by which
we count time remember their passing.

I do not know if the walnut tree in the yard
remembers its planting and pruning or if
the oak remembers its climb toward the stars.

I do not know if the squirrel remembers where
she hid the walnuts of winter or if the sparrows
remember their spring nests in the snows.

I do not know if the air remembers October
of if the night remembers the sun or if
the garden remembers its squash and roses.

Is the great white pine aware it is always green.
Do the hummingbirds remember my trumpet vine
or bees the clover I sowed just for them?

Perhaps the reason for our birth is to see,
hear, smell, taste and feel and remember
the season's rolling changes.

Perhaps salvation is different than anyone expects,
perhaps it depends on the answer to the question:
"What can you tell me about October?"

Morsel

5:55 a.m. I look out
at the world, cloudy, rain beading
and rolling off the windows in the
in the motel, my car in the handicap
space at Sleep Inn, Urbana.

The Interstate is rumbling,
the previous occupant's alarm
goes off at 6 with thunderous
statikiky music and cannot be stopped
until I tear the cord from the wall.

Restless in the night, a man shouting
"bitch" next door woke me. An insolent,
greedy machine repeated endlessly
"please deposit additional funds to
obtain your selected choice" until money
rattled and clicked: "Good choice, sir!"
I dream of a perpetual money
machine issuing tax-free dollars,
my children safe and alive praising
their dad for being a good provider.

Where are the lust dreams, dreams
of athletic success? The dream-maker
sends me images of a sailing hawk
watching others contending in their lives.
Occasionally the hawk swoops down
on some chipmunk, mole or other rodent
morsel, taking it unawares. There is
a feeling in the dream that I am a morsel
to be taken by something watching me.

6:05 a.m. I look out at the morning world
of cars passing through Illinois on their
way to Indiana, Iowa, Missouri through
thousands of acres of corn and beans where
millions of trembling morsels are
nuzzling one another in their
nests, grateful for another day.
Breathing. Waiting. Watching.

Body of Words

The haulers came to bear away my body
of work, 27 overfilled letter-size
boxes of words, piled in the drive,
a teetering five feet high, six feet wide,
to a rugged solid depth of seven feet,
my flesh become word, evidence of
the fire in my head, the fire in my heart
as I preached and practiced challenge
and consolation, urging respect for the
mystery of why there is any world at all
and appreciation for the mixed gift
of life and the beauty of the human.

Topping the pile were the prayers,
meditations, letters, articles, eulogies,
benedictions and the journals.

Here are records of the times in which
I lived: century of total war, holocaust,
numbed years of nuclear terror, economic
change, explosion of sexual freedom.
All my efforts at reform of society are there:
the battles in Birmingham and Selma,
protests of Viet Nam in Washington,
the long howl of protest against
murder as a way to improve the world.

There is also the record of being
a liberal in an illiberal society,
fighting the triumph of the arrogance of
corporate money-driven authoritarians.

My congregations tired of the summons
to battle and I learned to listen
to *their* hurts and buffetings, to discover
that each week there came those
facing illness, job loss, death, divorce,
jail, hounded by creditors, abused by
social workers, debt gnawing at their
guts, feeling powerless, hurt and angry.

My listeners were also the cheated,
discounted, the dull, the ignorant, drunks,
dopers, the mad, the crazed, the poor in
spirit and those full of grief, mourning.
I walked in their shadowed valleys
with them for they were me and I them.

He came week after week for years,
an undergraduate sitting in church,
filled with wise professors listening,
never greeting me at the door and
then he came no more...but wrote:

"I came to church to stay alive, to find
reason to live and every week you said
some word, told some joke, told a story
that I used to hold off the hungry black dog
 that walked with me the other six days.
I am alive. Thank you."

I preached hope, gratitude, forgiveness
and the possibility of new life—zest in
living—starting over after every failure
knowing we are always being born,
always growing, always able to make
a choice for love of those given us to love.

The team of haulers leafed through
the sermons casually, pausing in their work
to see what strange business I was discarding.
Several of the printed sermons were
folded and slipped into pockets.

The truck pulled away carrying my
body of words now consigned to fire.
I stood bereft, tears clotting my eyes:
Ashes, ashes, we all fall down.

Buying My Coffin

I bought my coffin today
meeting with the carpenter
to see his designs. The man loves
wood, the smell and feel of it,
and loves to shape and form it
into benches, bookcases and coffins.

So first we needed to choose a wood.
He suggests Indiana natives like poplar,
ash, pine, oak, walnut or sassafras.
I chose the velvety-smooth sassafras.

I thought sassafras was a bush,
the roots of which make a tea
to cure colds and fevers and to
warm you on cold winter nights.
It is also a potent way to rid
your house of rancid mustiness.

The coffin will open to double
as a bookcase of eight shelves.
It will hold 200 or more books
of variable sizes or one fully
grown man of 210 lbs—me.

I rub my cheeks on the smooth
board and feel I my nether cheeks
could rest comfortably on this
wood for as long as necessary.
Its lightly fragrant. The grain tells
the story of its years in the forest,
fat years of rain and growth and lean
years which make the wood stronger.

As a bookcase I will fill it with my
favorites, books by friends, books I
have written, books I love, reminding
me daily that I will die so I will live
pressing forward into the unknown
confident it will be wood-solid.

After She Went Away

After she went away the
house was too big, lonely
everything banged too loudly.

How can there be such
emptiness, such sullen,
sour, screaming silence?

Music cannot cure the vacant.
TV news' talking heads are
just as hollow as my house.

Time is tired, tedious.
Who knew how a woman
fills a house. makes it alive?

I try humming as she did
cooking her recipes but
the taste renews her absence.

Dust covers all now: quilts,
tables, silverware, dishes,
lamps, the plants, even me.

I bathe using her berry-scented
soap and shampoo, the tiny bath
becomes spacious emptiness.

I fill the quiet with angry sobs
and furious tears—some rageful
roaring around, stomping, cursing.

I yearn and long for restoration of that
mystery of woman, which can make
a house and the man in it alive again.

Under My Mother's Pillow

Under my mother's pillow is a key, a book and
a carton of Lucky Strikes in the green pack.

There is no father falling from the 20th street Viaduct.
No frozen hands from rinsing turnip greens on frosty morns.
No roomers with their hands up her dress, pressing her hard.
No Bible ragged from reading and study.
No flower-sack skirts gussied up with ribbons.

The key is to the house in Jefferson Hills
that she will never return to lost in the
Great Depression and her father's death.

There are no red sandals cutting into her feet
after fourteen hours of tromping from store
to store applying for jobs her sixteenth birthday,
the day after Christmas 1936.
No cheesecake pictures of the girl with the
Coca-Cola Bottle Shape—Miss Tarrant City.1938.
No husband old enough to be her father.
No little boys pulling and tugging at her.

The book "You Can Be a Teacher" makes
the pillow lumpy and hard but her three
children lived that dream for her.

There are no "Meatless Tuesdays" or Sunday meatloaf
extended with bread crumbs, kraut and Heinz ketchup.
No roses or Victory Garden, no DVD player,
no computer, no $8000 Viking stove to heat water.
No packet of love letters, no proof she was a Democrat.
No Citizen of the Year Award or sign she loved flowers.

She smoked the cigarettes to the end.
In hospice where she could give herself
morphine on demand she said "I want to go home
so I can smoke."

No philosophy under her pillow.
No post-modern ideas, no evidence that this was
Freud's century, no theory of the self.
No packet of poems stitched with red thread,
testament to her passion and intellect.
No complaints, no whining regrets.

Star in My Blue Heaven

Now that we know the universe is eternal
should we capitalize Universe?
13.7 billion years old, will last forever
(...world without end)
It is big, lots of stars, galaxies, planets, moons,
but most it is "dark matter" and "dark energy."
It is flat too, spread out like Kansas
for as far as the telescopes can see.
Cosmology becomes astronomy.
Astrology soldiers on but
don't ever ask an astronomer
"What's your sign?" although they
tend to be Taurus and Gemini, go figure?
I named Auriga RA 6h 24SD 39 28'
for my love, the star in my blue heaven.
I will go to her star when I die.

Katrina, Unfolding

My storm is quiet now.
After the winds,
after the rain,
after the flying
garbage cans,
the shingles,
the trees loosed
upon the waves—

I hear the sloshing
of water downstairs
and out on the streets,
a soprano saxophone,
strange, eerie, maybe
just in my head.

I lay in my warm bed
getting ready to worry
about the cat, Molly,
and Tom of course,
the rugs, my kitchen.
I am not hungry yet.

I take this moment
to just listen
to lapping water
and music from nowhere.

Is the world ended?
For now, I listen to water
and wind, the meanness
gone out of it.

I listen, while
water moves in rhythm.
I am dry, cozy in bed.
I cannot cry yet.

Much is lost, the future
uncertain but comfortable
with uncertainty I rest in
the wild-hearted world
in a bed where children were made,
where I gave myself to a man
I fear floats in ragged rumpled
waters on Melpomene Street.

My city blown away
while I still and quiet
my heart and listen
to what is unfolding. Soon
I will unfold myself too.

The Green Jar

She remembers her mother
in bed with Buck,
her father looming,
waving the coal-black gun.

He shouts: "I am going
to walk around the block.
If you are here when I get back,
I will kill you both."

Buck and mother scuttled away
leaving her with the wet-diapered
baby shaking and rattling his bed,
yelling for "sister, sister."

She is left, abandoned to come
home from school each day to
a vacant house filled with squeaks
settling and her mother's absence.

She hears scrabbling, scratching
and squeals from the basement where
her dolls live, stored, tucked away.
Twelve is too old for dolls.

She wanders the rooms touching
what her mother may have
touched. In the chifforobe she feels
among the boxer shorts the hard gun.

With a cracked china cup she
spreads white rice on a cookie sheet.
She salts it. She sticks her head
into the oven to light the hissing gas.

She eats the hard parched rice
off the end of her index finger,
slowly, deliberately, one at a time,
savoring the salt-burnt kernels.

With that finger she sneaks tips
of thick golden forbidden honey from
the green jar, gathering some sweetness
from the spoiled and bitter house.

Jocasta

Laius took the baby from me.
He was mine as much as his.
I watched as they pierced the heel
of the child who cried out as I cried out.
They did not want him to be
able to run away from the wolves
when he was set out to die. He
was mine, my flesh, I grew him,
I carried him and birthed him.

Because of the damned oracle,
the crazed bitches open at both
ends, never mothers themselves,
their smoky predictions warning
the boy would kill his father, my
child is taken to the mountain to die.

That boy lay between us
in the marriage bed all the years
of our life together. I heard the cry
of my child in every sexual taking.
My outcry always released tears
for my lost, murdered boy.

When the handsome one came,
the one who unriddled the Sphinx,
who brought order to Thebes, who
acted so audaciously, I saw Laius
in him—quick to anger, quick to act.

I desired this beautiful man. When he
asked my brother Creon for me,
my heart sprang to receive him
in my bed, delight at holding him, loving
the dark-eyed little boy in the man.
I saw his limp from the first, it ever so
slight. Joyfully I bathed those feet in
silver basins, at the heels cross-marked.
Yes, I remembered the oracle.

Plague is destroying Thebes, The murderer
of the King must be found. The shepherd's
tell him it is he who fulfilled the Oracle
and killed Laius at the place three roads meet.

Citizens scream for deliverance storming
the palace, shouting and torching, tables
and beds overturned, wails of the
children, servants cowering. I let down
my hair to its fullest length, weave
and wrap it into a rope to hang
myself writhing over our marriage bed.

King Oedipus comes to find my body, takes
the brooches that close my gown, stabbing
and tearing out his eyes, bawling like a
wolf gnawing a leg tangled in a trap.
Blind the King of Thebes limps out
of the city guided by his daughter-sisters.

Stone Lion

I am at a Buddhist retreat house in Bhutan in a gathering of
big shot Buddhist teachers from all over the world. They do not
know me so they assume I am one of them.

Dressed in robes they are arguing over who should give the
dharma talk. I am in my scruffy mud-spattered blue jeans, plaid
shirt and heavy boots just listening to conversation when one
of the leaders points at me and announces:

"He is sitting quiet. He should do it."

Never one to hang back I stand and give them the Stone Lion Lesson.

> In the middle of the night as the sun rises
> the lion emerges from his cave and roars.
> The blind see and the deaf hear clearly.
> Do you understand this?
>
> Cast a fishing line of a thousand feet
> into the ocean of space and watch clouds
> disappear, waves settle, coral grow,
> fish, whales, sharks and dragons sleep.

Load the ship with the moon, pull oar
and depart on the longest journey.
Ride the soaring goose around the world.
With utmost patience one becomes a sage.

They laugh when I tell them I am a lumberjack come to cut trees in
the forests of Bhutan.

Yunnan Triple Delight

We came at last, over the mountains,
to Gao Chai Kew and to Lake Tung Ting
where the poet Mo Fu celebrated and courted
his beloved Gai Woo, she of the broccoli
eyes and garlic mouth, hot and sour, her eyes
promising double happiness while coyly
rejecting the poet's honey-smooth words. This
is the way of courting and love in Kunming.

On the lake the Wor Shu ducks swim freely.
General Tso is far away but Mo Fu lays
the triple delight strategy of dragon meets
phoenix—spicy and hot. Gai Woo
and Mo Fu meet in the fierce duck dance.
Hot and sour becomes cool and sweet.

Day on Red Mountain

Millions of wildflowers,
suncup, fireweed, clover, vetch,
sedum, lupines, chokecherry.
I pick a dark crimson rose.
I see phlox and fairie slippers,
mule's ear and purple crazyweed.

Birds juking. jinking, jetting,
song answering song, delighting
in eating the seed heads of coneflowers.
Tiny bees fumble and tumble the flowers.
Surely this is heaven for them. Bees
and the honey of life poured out heals
even the most stubborn, clinging grief.

Sun and flowers, bees and birds,
I walk with strong legs, the years falling
away with every step, peace in each step.

A wailing sound hovers over the field,
The sound is sweet and clear and then
what the hell—there she is—naked—standing
in a crop of daisies the clarinetist answering
the birds, weaving, davenning, her eyes
closed to sharpen hearing, oblivious to
everything but the music, in ecstatic rapture.

I listen to the shape of the sounds
their duet penetrates and spins me,
Her clarinet tails off, the birds go quiet.

I want to speak to her but fear
to break the mood of exquisite happiness.
She is lovely and unguardedly erect.
She puts her instrument in the case and
twists down the crooked mountain trail.

The Art of Shining Shoes

My father, the old shoe dog, taught me
how to shine new shoes. It was the one
discipline of art he taught me.

A new pair of shoes, after you've tried
them on, should not be street worn until
shined with the best shoe polish available.

Inspect the shoe, wipe it free of all dust.
Apply polish thinly over the leathers,
buff to a high gloss with a soft cloth.

Repeat and dress the sole's edge darkening
the sole at the arch so there will be no flash of
whited leather when you are marching or dancing.

When you have shined them, protecting
them from rain, rocks, knocks and scuffs
you are then worthy to wear them.

Do this, he said, until the art and beauty
of the cobbler and his shoe is a part of you.

Continental Connection Flight 3407

"Fifty die in ice and fog on
a cold Friday night outside Buffalo."
-New York Times, February 15, 2009

A plane screams down on a house.
Human smoke pours out of the blaze
so intense it cannot be put out, hoses
freeze, the flames seen for miles.

Fifty families begin to reorder their lives.
Memorial services must be arranged,
obituaries readied, relatives called, closets emptied,
death certificates obtained, the urgent clamor of
lawyers listened to or rebuffed.

Lustrous time for raging about the way this
world is organized—shining death coming so soon
and lasting so long.

Bob's "Bills" tickets likely languish at "will call,"
Sandra's seat at the Met will go to someone else.
Another Cantor will sing at Temple Beth Am,
Clarissa will not pick up her son for soccer,

Sean's daughter will never hear her dad's voice.
John's daughter will have no one to give her away.
Coleman's last guitar solo has been played.
Matilda's sons now go to find their missing father.
Lorin's garden tiller will rust out this year.

Oh, if we could have known them we would have
loved them, so various, so rich, so promising.
We have now just the calm souls of the dead—
no more fear, no more dread—just dead.

There are tears of pain because something sweet
and indelible has gone out of fifty worlds.
To hold death at bay we speak the well wrought
ancient words, listen to personal stories,
hear music reaching up to the skies, and no
matter how truthful and apt they leave
us wandering through a night of ice and fog.

Baton

I remember when the *baton*
was what a conductor used to lead
the orchestra at the old civic auditorium.
He lifted the *baton* and when it came
down, music flooded the hall all the
way to the salt-glazed southern moon.

Now the *baton* is what our torturers use
against tight-lipped suspects of terrorism.
The *baton* can be made to bash soft
flesh and hard heads, to punch at the belly
and the groin, to mount a throttlehold, or
to slug a man who fights back.
The men use the *baton* but the women

of the new model army have their own
original techniques for the children
of Allah. Menstrual blood
smeared across the face makes
the closed-mouthed recalcitrant talk
or she'll unbutton her blouse and
rub her tits all over the young bound

prisoner—until his secrets leak
like a cracked egg.
She dances toward him
removing her tampon conducting
it as her special *baton*, threatening
to ram it in his mouth.
The crocheted blood-soaked rag
makes his cock shrink in shock,
the smoky plum of her vulva,
the terror of it coming for him
a music he's never heard.

Terminal Madness

On Learning of a Certain Poetry Competition
Celebrating a New Airport Terminal
in Indianapolis, Indiana in Which
Box Cutters, Fire, Flames, Aircraft Wreckage,
Blood, Gore, Dead Bodies, Coffins, Bombs,
Sexually Aggressive Imagery, Masked Figures,
Tornados, Lightning, Thunder Storms,
Rain or Any Other Forms of Inclement Weather
Are NOT Appropriate for Inclusion

It is madness to write
a rinky-dink poem
about an airport, glorifying it,
as if, like a waiter
dishing up spaghetti,
one could achieve a poem
worthy of being engraved,
to amuse, encourage or enchant
travelers forced to fly.

Terminal madness!

It is a functional place,
but barely so—a place of
bureaucracy, insolent machines,
humiliation, tedium and fear.

A perfect blend
of the stupidities
and irrationalities
of capitalism
and the touted evils

of government, the public-
private partnership cliché
with its petty charges,
lines interminable,
the rent-a-cop
civil servants who
resent you,
despise their jobs,
despise the absurdist
enterprise of 'security,'
snatching away tweezers,
pencils, finger-nail files,
making such things a Federal Case.
Searching grandmothers
who have never flown,
forcing them to remove their shoes.
Wands wander over
the body and they hold
the threat to search all body cavities.

All jokes and off-hand
comments are forbidden
(no contempt may be shown
or uttered about the
contemptible enterprise) or
they will throw your ass
on the ground shouting
into their body mikes
'We've got a situation here!'

The hideous food,
the uncomfortable chairs,
the blaring television is
sacrosanct emitting
continuous idiotic news
of violence, bombs, disasters,
(but I cannot include these in the
poem) or stop the black noise of Fox News.
(Signs warn: 'Do Not Turn off TV').

Planes are late, flights canceled
with no explanation, but there

are endless repetitious warnings
about parking, leaving bags unattended.
Madness! It engenders a windy
melancholy that is terminal,
a dozen crises an hour
of misplaced tickets,
lost children, spilled drinks,
pocketbooks left behind,
bags set down and carried away,
tedium piled on tedium
and nothing to be done.
No poetry is left.

Altered Life

Edith, my daughter, artist, librarian,
wrote in her own hand in her
journal, an altered book:

"I did not fall,

        I jumped.

My life
       was slipping away.
I
  was

     dying,
     d
      i
       s
        a
         p
          p
        e
        a
         r
        i
             n
            g.

Much to my chagrin, I woke up.
Now what?"

These are inscribed, nay graved,
upon the page after her first
attempt at self murder.

Next page: "Everything has its own beauty."

Last words in the book:

"Someday

you'll look back

and laugh."

Not yet.

Blackbird sings into the night,

Hawk soars above,

Catbird keeps jabbering,

While the honeybees are
d
  i
   s
    a
     p
      p
    e
    a
    r
    i
        n
       g.

The Dead Show

She was born Uptown in the good time 1950s
on Fat Tuesday in Baptist Hospital. Blue Cross
paid the bills and I called this girl "baby blue."
She was like New Orleans: full of zest for life,
a laughing girl who loved a pee-your-pants-good-time.

Later she was like New Orleans when the levees
broke, over-topped, and the city flooded. She
was flooded with rolling wave depression, hormones
rippling her body at midlife, menopause, numerous
numbing meds endlessly adjusted and balanced,
her back full of arthritis pain continuously, she
made a shout: "Hold! I choose to not be a victim."

She dashed off the suicide notes absolving others,
using the pages of her planner—one side for the
farewell notes, on the other her list of activities
for the week, all on acid-free pages.

Ready to let go she chose to drive to Pesotum—
a no-place place where she might not be found. There
she ate a month's supply of the butterfly blue sleep
potion Ambien, sixty brown tabs of Wellbutrin, some
unknown yellow pills and—bought especially for this,
from Walgreen—400 radiant orange enteric aspirin.

Found and taken to the hospital where she once
worked as a social worker, she raged against
her would-be saviors, tore at the cat's cradle of
tubes inserted in her veins, cursed the nurses,
screeched like a feral cat, mocking the staff.
Poseyed—hospital for tied down—she settled into
a deep and steady thrum of body-wracking breaths
until 'round midnight of the third day her heart
stopped. Machines screamed. life struggled out.
All the violence of modern dying was brought
to bear on her body—stabbing injections,
rib breaking pounding on the chest, electric shock
paddles that heave and jump the body in hopes
of restarting the heart. Blood, saliva, fluids from
the whirling tubes become spitting-angry snakes
that spatter the thirteen Code Blue respondents
crowding the room, watching helplessly. There was
no balm for this death. A man in scrubs asks if
I want them to "keep trying" as if some resurrection
might still be possible if we tried harder. "No," I said,
"if she comes back she will just 'keep trying' too."
I asked they stop the dead show and let her alone
knowing, as they did, that my girl was gone.

I look out into the star arched sky and hold
her hand as it turns icy-cold, watching her
body stiffen and turn blue—my flooded out girl
dashed about in hurricane winds of depressive sadness,
hopes drowned, her dreams washed out to sea.
Left behind is an empty city flooded and trashed.

Gift

Someone sees with my daughter's eyes
today staring out in green surprise,
to take in the golden glistening world
using the eyes of my glorious gone girl.

Will they see a world of pain and poverty?
Will they notice millions yearn to be free?
They may wonder who had these eyes before.
and why she doesn't have them anymore.

There is medicine in looking with new eyes
at flowers and trees waving at the sky.
Her eyes play with words and color,
delighting in this world like no other.

A stunning dazzlement is this gift of sight.
Edith's eyes now dancing through the night.

Ride of Her Life

Death came in his black mud-caked pick-up
offering her the ride of her life. He was
dark-eyed, pock-marked with duck's ass
pompadour like every bad-boy boyfriend
she'd ever ridden with through corn and
soybean fields of the Champaign County.

They drove to Papa Del's Pizza where
she had her first job, where she told off
the imperious pompous professors who left
a fifteen cent tip. She followed them down
the sidewalk throwing the nickel and dime
shouting: "Here, you forgot your change!"
Assertive woman at fifteen, not taking shit.

Over to the high school with its
"grit door," "jock door," "black door,"
where each day she entered teen-hell
but somehow closed with grades
for college and an award that mystified
all who knew her, "The Betty Crocker
Family Leader of Tomorrow Award."

They drove to the White Horse Tavern,
where she, drugs, boys and beer got together.
Then over to brick paved West Indiana Street
and 704, her home for thirteen years.

Across the Fourth Ward to Carle Park where
she was arrested for smoking marijuana
and got to see the inside of the city's jail.

They paused out front of Café Royale
her favorite coffee place but did not go in.
Then to the Presbyterian Church where
in Alcoholics Anonymous she got herself
sober with the help of a bunch of drunks.

At the public library she sobs for the
girl she was who loved books and drove the
bookmobile and read to children of every race.

They go past the homes of her friends,
the Kerasotes theater where she sold tickets.
They drive slowly past Jane Addams
School of Social Work where she sharpened her
passion to create social justice in this country.

From there to the Champaign County
Nursing Home where she worked for
five years and now feared she might
wind-up sitting and rocking, vegging out
in the timeless anterooms of pre-death.

They drove past all the places she lived
and worked, then down Green Street
to the Unitarian Church —a world
she never made, right past the Reed's
house, the teen-age hangout where she
was held down and forcibly fucked by a
certified sexual predator one sunny day.

Death, a sweet man, drove to her house
on Burlison where her marvelous daughter
sleeps and where in the backyard a stone cairn
of her lost child Nora Katherine is intact.

He is a kindly guide showing her the
transit of the life she lived and was leaving.
"Where are we going now?"
"Home" said rough-hewn Death,
"home where every one goes, the
place in your heart you most want to be."

He steps on the gas—burning rubber,
taking off like a bat out of Birmingham.

Veil of Silence

Her books are gathered for resale,
mostly dealing with anger, pain,
menopause, divorce, drugs for depression,
and techniques for living day to day,
books of uplift and positive thinking.

Take it easy.

    One day at a time.

Be grateful to every one.

Take a deep breath.

Turn arrows into flowers.

Pray for the sons of bitches.

All useful counsel, and beautiful too
when life is fresh and glowing
but now silly shallow shards of graffiti.

Her spirit lives—bringing door-slamming
rage and blue bitter tears, denial and
acquiescence, acceptance and questions.

There is a thin veil between worlds
made of silence and mystery,
evanescence of the full moon,
the flight of birds, wind, falling leaves,
the death of flowers, breaking of glass,
stopping of engines, stillness as sirens fade
and barking dogs go quiet in the night.

Red Memory

She is dead these last months but
I have memory of her in the song of the goldfinch,
the scrabbling chatter of starlings and grackles,
the black capped chickadees,
the red-throated Harris sparrows.

Yes, and in the cry of geese, wondrous
moan of longing in the loon.
and in every sure and lovely
object—her worry beads, the journal,
the earrings, the small red knife, the violent
red blooms of the Christmas cactus which
just now makes a show for all to see.
Poor world, without Edith.

Staggered

Some books
 should be open
 to the sky.

No walls—only wonders—
 everyone who hears
 the word is fed.

The adornments of lilies
 and the birds
 come alive.

Seeds, soil, sun
 and water become
 upspringing wheat

and plumped grapes bursting,
bread and wine
 not far behind.

Body and blood transformed
 as we drink
 the wine of astonishment.

LaVergne, TN USA
09 December 2009
166318LV00001B/1/P